sheep

joy

Pebble® Plus

book

What Is a NOUN?

park

Maria

birds

by Sheri Doyle

family

Consulting Editor: Gail Saunders-Smith, PhD

PARTS OF SPEECH

CAPSTONE PRESS
a capstone imprint

Pebble Plus is published by Capstone Press,
1710 Roe Crest Drive, North Mankato, Minnesota 56003.
www.capstonepub.com

Library of Congress Cataloging-in-Publication Data
Cataloging-in-publication information is on file with the Library of Congress.
ISBN 978-1-62065-126-1 (library binding)
ISBN 978-1-4765-1730-8 (ebook PDF)

Editorial Credits
Jill Kalz, editor; Heidi Thompson, designer; Marcie Spence, media researcher; Laura Manthe, production specialist

Photo Credits
Alamy Images: Marvin Dembinsky Photo Associates, 9, 11, Rick & Nora Bowers, 19; Capstone Studio: Karon Dubke, cover (boy), 21; Shutterstock: Becky Stares, cover (sign), Evgeni Stefanov, 13 (top), Floris Slooff, 15 (top right), Le Do, cover (ball), majeczka, 15 (left), Maks Narodenko, cover (bananas), Maxim Slugin, 7, Olga Sapegina, 5, Stephen Meese, 15 (bottom right), Uryadnikov Sergey, 13 (bottom), WA van den Noort, 17

Note to Parents and Teachers

The Parts of Speech set supports English language arts standards related to grammar. This book describes and illustrates nouns. The images support early readers in understanding the text. The repetition of words and phrases helps early readers learn new words. This book also introduces early readers to subject-specific vocabulary words, which are defined in the Glossary section. Early readers may need assistance to read some words and to use the Table of Contents, Glossary, Read More, Internet Sites, and Index sections of the book.

Printed in the United States of America in North Mankato, Minnesota.
092012   006933CGS13

Table of Contents

Meeting Nouns

Say hello to nouns!

A noun is one part

of speech. It names

a person, place,

or object.

park

bird

girl

5

A noun can name an idea or feeling. The words "love," "sadness," and "happiness" are nouns.

The kids jump for <u>joy</u>.

A noun is either common
or proper. Most nouns are
common nouns. They name
general people, places,
or objects.

farm

girl

turkey

sheep

goats

9

Proper nouns name
special people, places,
or objects. They begin
with a capital letter.

Sunny Farm

Maria

Arnold

Ollie

Ming

Bing

11

More Than One

What if there are
two or more objects?
The word "plural" means
more than one. Most plural
nouns end in "s" or "es."

The <u>bird</u> sits on the <u>branch</u>.

The <u>birds</u> sit on the <u>branches</u>.

13

Some nouns are irregular.
They don't add "s" or "es"
to become plural. They
change their letters, or
they don't change at all.

one sheep

many sheep

one mouse

many mice

one deer

many deer

15

Sometimes a group

of people, animals,

or objects is treated

as one noun. "Family"

and "team" are group nouns.

The <u>class</u> sees a <u>family</u> of zebras.

It's Mine!

Possessive nouns have or own something.
They end in an apostrophe or an apostrophe plus "s" to show ownership.

The <u>opossum's</u> babies hold on.
singular

The <u>babies'</u> heads are small.
plural

The world is made of nouns.

You're sitting on a noun.

You're using nouns to read.

And now you've finished

reading a noun!

Glossary

apostrophe—a punctuation mark used to show ownership or missing letters in a contraction

common noun—a word that names a general person, place, or object

irregular—not going by a rule or common method

object—anything that can be seen and touched; a thing

plural—more than one

possessive—showing ownership or belonging

proper noun—a word that names a special person, place, or object

Read More

Heinrichs, Ann. *Nouns.* Mankato, Minn.: Child's World, 2011.

Shaskan, Trisha Speed. *If You Were a Plural Word.* Word Fun. Minneapolis: Picture Window Books, 2010.

Walton, Rick. *Herd of Cows! Flock of Sheep!: An Adventure in Collective Nouns.* Layton, Utah: Gibbs Smith, 2011.

Internet Sites

FactHound offers a safe, fun way to find Internet sites related to this book. All of the sites on FactHound have been researched by our staff.

Here's all you do:

Visit *www.facthound.com*

Type in this code: 9781620651261

Super-cool stuff! Check out projects, games and lots more at **www.capstonekids.com**

Index

Word Count: 174
Grade: 2
Early-Intervention Level: 21